Dear Martha

Thank you so
Support. Keep changing the
World through music!

Love And Light

Joe Pound

Lots of love,

Joe Pound
x

Copyright © 2015 Joe Pound

Roots Of Love Publishing
All rights reserved.

ISBN-13: 978-1517472634
ISBN-10: 1517472636

By love, for love

This is for all the energy that has been passed onto me through great souls. You are the writers, I am simply the transcriber. If it were not for the countless number of great people who I have in my life, my words would not be in existence. My words are a product of people and experiences and therefore, I cannot take credit for this book. From the deepest corners of my heart, I owe the world to all of you. My greatest wish is that this book becomes a source of inspiration, motivation, laughter, energy and above all, love for whoever reads it. May this book, which has become a part of me, become a part of you.

Love And Light

You are a woman,
That alone is everything.
You were already a completed poem the
Moment you left your mother's womb.

I can't help but wish I was your perfume,

Clinging myself to every crevasse of your skin.

All but a breath of my name is all I need to hear from

You in order to build my nest in the roots of your love.

I miss the future that is destined for us.

Contradiction,

I Know.

But you make me believe the impossible.

I would move mountains just to be a kink in your hair,

The spoon that feeds you,

Or the energy of your softness that is spoken so loudly.

Love And Light

I dream of your Apartment.

3am.

Bloodshot eyes.

Tongues lined with the near empty bottle of rum.

Tearful laughter.

Piled together on your maroon rug.

The stars may have been outside,

But we had the whole world in that room.

- Nneka

Joe Pound

Only my words

And

3am

Know my secrets.

The Seas purpose is to keep flowing;
As is yours,
As is mine.

- *'A Rolling Stone Gathers No Moss'*

Empty 'I love you's'
And sorrowful kisses
Are all we have left.

- Once Rope, Now Thread

I hope you realise that
It would take the view of
10,000 sunsets to equate to
The beauty that i see in you.

Love And Light

I always expected the meaning of life to be an intangible
Concept.
How pleasantly surprising it is,
To hold the meaning of life
In my arms
And to further seal my purpose
With a kiss.

Joe Pound

If beauty is in the arms of who can hold her,
Then poetry is in my fingers
And I can write her.

I still remember hearing your heartbeat for the first time.
It is the rhythm to my favourite song
And I don't intend to stop the music anytime soon.

- Music To My Ears

Joe Pound

Grass as my bed,
A pillow full of daisies.

Warm summer nights,
It feels good to be lazy.

-Hazy Days

Love And Light

Being a six year old and eagerly awaiting
On a Christmas morning to unwrap a present
Cannot compare to my desire to
Open your mind
And discover what is inside.

- The Greatest Gift

It is not only I who is in love tonight.
Even the stars are falling for you.

- 2:16am, Shooting Stars

I believed that the collision of our hearts would form
A chemical reaction that scientists could only dream of.

Looking back,
I can't quite understand how I believed that the collision
Of our hearts would cause anything other than
A crash,
A wreckage.

- Disillusioned

Joe Pound

Although I may claim that I wear my
Heart on my sleeve,
At times,
I find it all too easy to
Keep my sleeves rolled down
Cuff linked to my wrists
To deter anyone from entering.

Love And Light

Tell me you love me once more,
But this time,
Do it without moving your lips.

I want to hear it through your eyes
And your soul.

If I cannot feel it,
My love,
I will have to leave.

- Your 'I Love You's' Have Been Empty For Too Long

I closed your legs,
Then proceeded to make love to you.

The first time for it to happen in that sequence.

It was then that I realised
That making love
Is so much more than a physical adventure.

Love And Light

I wouldn't have to smoke,
And I'd still get high from you.

I wouldn't have to live,
But I'd still die for you.

Joe Pound

If I were a bird with the opportunity of flight,
I wouldn't take it.

For to be in your nest
Is the only place I desire to be.

Love And Light

Anyone can tell you you're beautiful,
But it takes that special person to realise
How 67 strands of your hair
Fall so poetically over your right eye.

- Attentive Beauty

You were too precious for this earth,
Rest in peace
And may heaven know your worth.

- Kay

It's amazing how you can just sit there
And speak to me in a way
That words fail to achieve.

Yes we made love,
But not in the traditional sense.

We found love.
Created
And
Patented love.

Love belongs to
And is owned by us.

- Copyright

Love And Light

They say you only truly miss someone
When they're dead and gone,

But even when you go to the shop to buy milk
I yearn for your presence.

Joe Pound

I don't see a future with you,
I see eternity.

Love And Light

Relax my dear…

Let's put our feet up

And embrace the world

Resonating with our heartbeats.

- Silence

Joe Pound

You. You. You. You. You. You. You. You. You. You.
You. You. You. You. You. You. You. You. You. You.
You. You. You. You. You. You. You. You. You. You.
You. You. You. You. You. You. You. You. You. You.
You. You. You. You. You. You. You. You. You. You.
You. You. You. You. You. You. You. You. You. You.
You. You. You. You. You. You. You. You. You. You.
You. You. You. You. You. You. You. You. You. You.
You. You. You. You. You. You. You. You. You. You.
You. You. You. You. You. You. You. You. You. You.
You. You. You. You. You. You. You. You. You. You.
You. You. You. You. You. You. You. You. You. You.
You. You. You. You. You. You. You. You. You. You.
You. You. You. You. You. You. You. You. You. You.
You. You. You. You. You. You. You. You. You. You.
You. You. You. You. You. You. You. You. You. You.
You. You. You. You. You. You. You. You. You. You.
You. You. You. You. You. You. You. You. You. You.
You. You. You. You. You. You. You. You. You. You.

Love And Light

You.

- Everything, A One Word Story

Joe Pound

Blessed is life,

When the sun rises by day

And sets by night.

I hope you realise that it would take the view of
10,000 sunsets to equate to the beauty that I see in you.

I sat silent,

Closed my eyes

And envisioned the most beautiful place in the world.

It's funny…

Palm trees and exotic beaches entered my thoughts,

But I would choose no other place

Than the paradise of your mind.

Love And Light

All words have been spoken.

All songs sung.

All poems written.

Yet I am a blank canvas.

Longing to be created with the colours of your mind.

Joe Pound

Love.
What we live for,
What we die for
And everything in between.

Love And Light

I love it when you speak to me with your fingertips.

Joe Pound

Some may say that
Music, writing, poetry and art
Aren't realistic life pursuits,

But without these,
Life would be no pursuit at all.

Don't be scared of what you might say,
Be terrified of what you might not say.

- Vulnerability

You looked down.

Saw the bloodstains

Clinging to the bed sheets.

Your spiritless face told me

How overcome you were

With embarrassment.

I felt sick.

In my stomach.

My bones.

My spirit.

I felt sick because I couldn't understand

Why your eyes were apologising to me.

Why society ingrained into you that you should feel

Ashamed from your period.

We took the sheet off together

(Continued)

And threw it in the washing machine with the rest of the
Dirty clothes.
You seemed confused as to why I didn't take the other
Clothes out first.
I wanted you to know that I didn't give a shit.
The blood from your vagina is no more unclean than the
Sweat from my t-shirt.

Over hot coffee we both expressed how your period
Should be celebrated.
How it indicates your capabilities of reproducing.
What a blessing.

Your period is sacred.
An indicator of life.

We never discussed this moment again,
But it is one that I hold close to my heart.
Thank you for your holiness.

Joe Pound

As one door is closes,
Another may open.

But with all these second
Chance opportunities,
I'm scared that my once
New door
Will soon fall from its hinges.

Love And Light

It doesn't have to be autumn
For the leaves to fall for you,
Nor night for the stars
To fall at your feet.

Look at the way the birds sing for you.
The way the sun shines for you.

Mother nature is in awe of you.

Delve yourself into my lungs.
Etch your voice into my rib cage.
I want to speak of you
With each and every breath.

I have an appetite for your soul,
Feed me!

- Gluttony

"   "

- What about the words left unsaid?
  What about the moments that leave us speechless?
  What if there are emotions, feelings and moments that
  Can never be turned into poetry, books or music?
  What if silence is the most beautiful voice we can
  Speak?

Love And Light

Embrace pain as tightly as you hold love.
For this is the key to acceptance.
Sometimes the water will flow against you.
At times, fight it.
At times, feel it.

With patience,
You will surely feel life flow with you.

Joe Pound

In essence of a fine wine, I will swirl your moans around
My palate
And learn how every part of my tongue is designed to
Become accustomed to your flavours.

Although tempting,
I will resist the urge to gulp you at once,
And in turn,
I will savour every droplet until the last one trickles down
My throat and into my stomach
Whilst my heavy sigh will gratefully suggest
That the pleasure was all mine.

Getting lost with you is where I find myself the most.

- Adventure

July 12th
The night the moon and stars
Quilted two forms of love
Into one fabric.

- Dear Umeh

Love And Light

Good morning world,
So grateful for the slice of crimson the sun
Offers me each morning.

Good morning soul,
Equally grateful for the struggles, that in turn,
Will no doubt blossom wisdom.

- Kaizen

Joe Pound

How strange,

To feel so free when trapped in your arms.

Love And Light

I didn't hear your voice,

I didn't have to.

Your eyes told me everything I needed to know.

No matter how tired my fingers,
They will always have the strength to write about you.

- My Love, My Love

Love And Light

With you,
>I'm learning.
>>To
>>>Fall
>>>>Without
>>>>>Holding
>>>>>>On.
>>>>>>>To be courageous without knowing
>>>>>>>If it will be my heart falling for you,
>>>>>>>>Or
>>>>>>>>>Break-ing
>>>>>>>>>Into
>>>>>>>>>>T wo.

'I miss you', I thought…
As I stared at you beside me
Wondering how you could be present,
Yet so absent,
At the same time.

Love And Light

Breathe in,
Breathe out.

Feel the air circulating in your lungs,
Feel your heart beating.

You are not only living,
You are alive.

Joe Pound

Don't allow a man to taste your dessert
If he's not willing to
Digest your
Starter
And
Mains.

Love And Light

Your superpowers amaze me.
I can't quite fathom your ability to
Transform from a person
To ink on my page
Within a matter of seconds.

Joe Pound

Silence is my first voice.

Love And Light

You were an ocean to me.
I was only a wave to you.

You were eager to ride with me at my peak,
But once I broke,
You found a new wave.

And there I remained,
A droplet in your all consuming ocean.

Joe Pound

All I can think about is you and what I'm going to eat
Next...
Oh wait,
They're the same thing.

Love And Light

She's something like my queen,
    Something like my earth.

    Something like my gift,
    Something like my curse.

Joe Pound

You whispered my name
And it echoed in the corners of my heart
That have been empty for years.

Time is of the essence.

Live simply.

Breathe deeply.

And let earth feel your presence.

Joe Pound

Good things come to those who wait,
Better things come to those who create.

Love And Light

Love.

The ability to be imprisoned,
Yet free.

Single,
Yet one entity.

Have absence,
Yet feel company.

They say you can be whoever you want to be.
So I chose,
Decided.

All I want to be,
Is me.

Love And Light

The sound that vacates your lips

Is the sound of

Every musical masterpiece

Playing at once.

- Keep Talking

My arms are tired of waiting to hold you.

- Distance

The wind blew
And the mountains echoed.

It was your name
And it always was.

- Calling

Joe Pound

Writing poetry is where you find both happiness and
Loneliness.

The ability to see stars during a storm
And feel liberated whilst in prison.

It's everything and nothing
And never one without the other.

It's a scary thought that we can end our lives at any
Given time that we choose…
What's even scarier,
Is that at any moment,
We also have the ability to start our lives.

Leave a legacy,
By all means, leave a legacy.
When you truly understand life and how little we have
Here in the grand scale of human existence,
You will no doubt feel an unprecedented need to
Leave a legacy.

Leave something for your children to inherit,
Leave something for future generations to develop.
Sing.
Dance.
Write.
Inspire.
Let it be known that you deserved your spot in life
And did what you could to leave a mark moulded by
Integrity, courage, determination, passion and above all,
Love.

Love And Light

There is no you,
There is no me,
Only we.

I love consuming you.

- Healthy Appetite

Love And Light

They may love your fruits,

But will they

Use any

Of their time

To water your roots?

- Don't Be Fooled

Joe Pound

I want to write about you,
But I don't know how to.

Three years together,
And I still don't know you.

Love And Light

I knew you were the one...

Not by your beautiful looks or your inspiring mind,
But by the way you poured coffee in the morning
And how you placed your hair band in your mouth
Before tying back your hair.

- The Little Big Things

Joe Pound

I always admired that trait in her…
How she never complained,
Yet always moaned.

Love And Light

You were never in my prayers,
But lord knows you were in my answers.

Joe Pound

I do not wish to be in front of you,
Nor behind you.

I wish to be beside you.
Where there is no power.
No ego.

Syncing our paths.
Syncing our heartbeats.

A place where both of us will feel the sun
And neither will fall behind in the shadows.

- Complement, Not Compete

Do not break her open in order to get to her core.
Nurture her.
Water her roots.
With time,
She will trust your patience
And break free from the soil
To present her flower to you.

- Earn Her Depth

Joe Pound

I want every portion of your skin
That you've ever
Cried over
To be on my lips.

Love And Light

Hidden in the darkest corners of my bitterness

Lies a beaten.

Torn.

Battered voice.

That quietly whispers,

'Come home'.

Joe Pound

I'm drinking more these days…
I had to find something to smother my lips
That were once occupied by your own.

Love And Light

Before you throw your words into the air,
Chew them.
Taste them.
Swirl them around in your mouth.
If they consist of the desired ingredients,
Release them.
Always give your words wings
Before you allow them to take flight.

Joe Pound

It will always be within the shivers of your skin
Where I will write my greatest poetry.

Love And Light

Some may have held a place in my heart,

But only you have swum

Through my veins

In order etch your name

Into the centre of my chest.

Joe Pound

Our greatest opportunities lie within our greatest fears.

Love And Light

I have no interest in being
A master of love making.
My only concern is
Mastering the language
Of the person with whom
I choose to lay with.

Joe Pound

Words won't leave my lips,
But I will still let my mouth do the talking.

- Cunnilinguist

Love And Light

It would be an honour to be
The very ground you walk on,
The air you breathe from,
Or the touch the moan from…

Sometimes, talking about nothing
Is the best something
You can give someone.

- My Energy Is Always Here For You To Talk To

Love And Light

Even after a physical breakup,
You can never leave a writer.

For that will be the beginning of their relationship
With you and their pen.

- Beginning After The End

Joe Pound

Sometimes there are

Conversations only your

Legs can start.

Love And Light

Don't emigrate your love to another's heart,
Become a dual citizen of love.

Love isn't about giving your heart another home,
It's about having the ability to travel
With the additional freedom to remain in your own nest.

- Freedom

A skip in my step,
A swing in my hips.

A rhythm in my heart,
Words from my lips.

Tender by touch,
Arms that hold.

26 years young,
Not one day old.

Blessed is my day,
Never taking one as a given.

A universe in my eyes,
A story to be written.

Love And Light

I didn't find poetry,

Poetry found me

And it came in the form of you.

Failing at something you love is
Worth more admiration
Than being successful at
Something you loathe.

Our courageous capacity
Must always be celebrated more
Than conforming to the mundane.

Relax,
It will come.

- Patience

The flower may have no smell,
But you can still feel its essence.

You may have gone,
But I can still feel your presence.

Love And Light

When I think of you,
I think not of perfection,
For that in itself is imperfect.

Instead,
I think of existence,
And how I no longer have to question it anymore.

- Im per-fect

Edure
　Endur
　　Endu
　　　End
　　En
　Enli
　Enlight
Enlighten

- Always Believe That The Road You Endure Will End With Enlightenment.

Love And Light

Honour God, follow your dreams.
Honour love, follow you heart.
Honour your mother, be graceful.
Honour yourself, be truthful.
Honour others, show empathy.
Honour life, show humility.

Grasp hold of your loneliness.

For solitude is where you will find the greatest company.

Love And Light

It's strange.

How we never have time for anything.

To read. To write. To sleep.

To run errands. To watch movies. To cook.

To relax. To visit friends. To travel.

Until we find love.

For love is timeless and is not bound by schedule.

- Timeless

Joe Pound

One day I took her for dinner,
The next,
I ate her for dinner.

Love And Light

If you feel like you're settling down
With someone when you commit,
Get out of there at the quickest possible time.

Commitment should give you
Thunderstorms
And
Rainbows.
Make you want to dive into the deepest oceans
And sing in the rain.

Commitment with the right person will make you
Climb the highest mountains and dance in the street.

It will make you do anything but settle.

People often look back and mourn how they let a
Good thing slip away.

I however,
Have the greatest pleasure in looking back
Knowing that I won the lottery
Without ever buying a ticket.

- Jackpot

Love And Light

My eyes had no vision until they met your gaze.
Thank you for my sight
And welcoming me to your world.

- Seeing

We became cats.
Timid.
Gentle.

When all we've ever known to be, are lions.
Powerful.
Alive.

We were left with no choice
But to leave the cage of our relationship.

- Empty Roar

Love And Light

If one person is oppressed,
We are all oppressed.

- Unity

Joe Pound

There are verbs to describe action,

Nouns to describe objects,

But what are failed to be taught,

Are 'being' words.

Be love.

Be conscious.

Be liberated.

Be spiritual.

Be courageous.

There are no in-betweens with these words;

You either are,

Or you are not.

Love And Light

If you're not accepting of immigrants,
Perhaps you should emigrate back to
Your mother's womb,
Or the hand that God created you with.

- We Are All Immigrants

Voices in my head always
Fail to transpire,
Therefore,
My silence will remain a barrier
To my heart's desire.

- I Wish I Had The Strength To Tell You

Love And Light

In creation of each one of us,

God gave us a song.

It is in our duty to sing it.

- Calling

For all her successes and everything she had to strive for,
I'm still wondering what she took her life for.

- Kay

Love And Light

In the midst of your desperation,

May you reap

Love.

Light.

And

Salvation.

I could be dead to the one's who I have loved,
But never the other way around.

- Physically Erased, Spiritually Marked.

Discover your purpose.

Uncover your talents.

Apply courageousness to the pursuit of fulfilment.

Joe Pound

We must always learn from mother nature.

For even when a tree dies,

It is covered by moss

In a blanket of appreciation.

Love And Light

I'm pulling on your shirt begging you not to go,
When I should be
Pulling on your hair begging you to come.

Joe Pound

There's
Earth.
Air.
Wind.
Fire.
And *you*.

All essential components to the earth's existence.

Love And Light

May you know your nature so well,
That if people proclaim otherwise
To who you truly are,
You can smile and only wish for them to have
The same knowledge of self that you possess.

As people,

We are learning that money is not the truest form of

Wealth and success.

However,

We still have more admiration for people who have

Money in their pocket

Over those

With love in their heart.

With arms that hold.

With a voice of truth.

With a belly of laughter.

We may understand it,

But little do we preach it.

Stop adding fuel to the fire we need to douse.

- The Wealth Remains In The Eyes Of A Person Who Is More Willing To Carry Love In Their Heart, Over Money In Their Pocket

Love And Light

I tried to open her eyes,
But I could only open her thighs.

She tried to open my mind,
But thoughts she could not find.

I spoke of emptiness through the voice of intimacy,
The lust to touch got the best of me.

Show her your ABC's before your D.

- Intellectual Before Sexual

Love And Light

You crawled across my notebook like a bug.
I squashed you.

You splattered across my pages forming words
With your mess.

You were dead to me,
But you still made poetry.

Joe Pound

The sun and moon know not to compete,
But to complement.

As one rises, the other admires.

They're aware that there is enough space in the sky for
Both of them.

Each of their light is needed in a unique and majestic
Way and one without the other can never complete their
Destiny.

They both succeed,
Because they both shine.

Love And Light

It's my culture to dry your eyes.

I want our
Minds to lay
Naked together
Whilst we
Expose our
Thoughts to
Each other's
Soul.

- Mind Sex

Love And Light

If he tries to eat you before you are ripe,
Make your fruits bitter.

That way,
He will never have the satisfaction of tasting
Your sweet nectar.

Joe Pound

Writing.
It helps you get love,
It helps you lose love.

Love And Light

My once was,
That never really was.

- Yesterday

Joe Pound

My life began

When you

Tortured my lips

With your kisses.

Love And Light

I write about you too easy.
I sometimes wonder how my pen can spill its ink
Before my mind spills its thoughts.

It's not fair on you.
Someone of such sacredness deserves their being
To be marinated and digested before consumption.

I write about you too easy.
But how could it be any different,
When you allow my pen to glide so freely.

Joe Pound

Feel my last breath,
As I seek death quietly.

My hopes, my dreams,
Buried six feet below me.

- Giving In

Feel my first breath,
As I begin life quietly.

My hopes, my dreams,
Blossoming inside me.

- Beginning

Fall
  A
   p
    a
     r
      t
Fall
  I
   n
    t
    o

    P
   l
  a
 c
e

Fall in love.

Love And Light

Dining with your partner
Shouldn't always include a knife and fork.
Sometimes you got to eat (her)
Without preparation.

- Recipes For Southern Cuisine

Joe Pound

What's magical by moonlight,
Is impossible by daylight.

It's bittersweet that something so strong
Can be lost with the wake of the sun.

Love And Light

You don't need to
Know the questions to
Find the answers.

The self is who we are.

The person is what other people know.

- Stay True To The *Self*

Love And Light

It's impossible to write about you
When all you do is leave me speechless…

Joe Pound

I wish for you to live your today's
How you imagine
Your tomorrow's to be.

I wish for your tomorrow's
To be today.

Love And Light

One day,

I really hope I can truly say I did it.

I went through

Hell.

Pain.

Fear.

Uncertainty.

And everything that was in my way,

But I did it.

- The Arena

Joe Pound

You are the bullet to my trigger.
I'm too dangerous when I'm with you,
But without you,
I'm nothing.

- Catch 22

Love And Light

If only my arms could reach through the
Time and distance
That separates us.

But my arms remain alone,
Crowded with emptiness.

I won't go back. I won't go back. I won't go back.
I won't go back. I won't go back.
I won't go back.

I went back.

I tasted the devil's nectar once more.

- (S) ex

Love And Light

Your 5 foot 3 frame stood below mine,
But you were above me in every way.
I *adore* you.

Gather your wisdom from yesterday and today.
Scatter it across the ocean.
Allow it to be washed up upon the shores of others
And be cherished in a new home.

- The Wealth Of Sharing

Love And Light

My identity is my own construction.
I am my parent's love.
I am God's creation.
I am mother nature's son.
My heart is Nigerian.
My soul is Caribbean.
My tongue is British.
My spirit is music.

My home is not a place,
It is who I am.

- Where I Am From

Joe Pound

Who would've thought that the fire
That we built our love from,
Would be the same fire
To burn our hearts to ashes.

Love And Light

The value of her breasts are in their ability to feed.
The value of her lips are in their ability to speak wisdom.
The value of her backside is in its ability to
Cushion her hard working body.
The value of her hips are in their ability to carry life.
The value of her vagina is in its ability to create life.

Clap for yourself.

Encourage your scars to be accepted.

Learn from your hips.

Paint the world with the curves of your existence.

Vibrate with your own energy.

Never wait on anyone regarding the

Acceptance of your

Mind.

Body.

Or

Soul.

You should always be your biggest fan.

Love And Light

I will risk tracing your body with my fingertips
Knowing that my touch
May be erased at any time.

Joe Pound

Do not be mistaken when people may not see
The greatness in you.

Where some may only see you as yellow,
You should always see yourself as golden.

Tread not heavy amongst mother nature,
She is always birthing.

Joe Pound

White privilege is formed by the blood of Black lives.
Until our last breath,
We must heal the wounds we once inflicted
And pray for forgiveness for
The scars that are left behind.

- A Pledge

Love And Light

I know your wings have been clipped many times over,
But I must remind you,
That through my eyes,
My dear,
You are always in flight.

- My Dear, The Sky Is Yours

Joe Pound

Travel with people,

You may encounter conflict and ego.

Travel with nature.

In woods.

With birds.

Up mountains.

You will experience nothing but friendship.

Love And Light

The book of our love has needed to be closed,
Yet we continue to read on
In hope of a happy ending.

- Un-rea-lis-tic

By seeing through the eyes of a bird,

We may realise that the hand that feeds us

Is the same hand that keeps us locked in our cage.

Our beauty may appeal to the majority,

But our greatest attribute will remain in our wings

With which we can fly.

We will remain enslaved if the person we are with

Fails to understand this.

- The Beauty Of Our Wings

I soon realised that the water you bathed me in
Was the same water you used to drown me.

I am too submerged,
But still I grasp for air
Knowing that I won't pierce the surface.

- Drowning

Joe Pound

The only time we should be allowed to open our mouths
Concerning the female body,
Is when they invite us at dine
At their Southern cuisine.

- A Message To Men

Love And Light

You made her wet?
Congratulations.
But realise that her body was already
70% water before you arrived.

- A Body Of Water

I struggle with the terms introvert and extrovert.
How can the uniqueness of seven billion personalities
Only fit into two boxes.

What about the extroverts who value their alone time,
Or the introverts who are great conversationalists?

You can be an introvert with one person,
Yet an extrovert with others.
You, I and we
Are anything but these terms.

We are explosions and silence.
Sunsets and thunderstorms.
Movement and stillness,
And everything in-between.

- INTROVERTS/*extroverts*

Love And Light

Let the sun be jealous of your shine.

Joe Pound

I hope one day you will be able to wash your body
Clean from my lustful fingertips
That have stained your body.

- Lustful Stains

Love And Light

Don't go down on her
If your intentions are to
Paddle in her waters,
You must submerge yourself.

- Swim

Joe Pound

My lips turned into sand and were met by your sea
Filtering through my every granule.
Gravity was no longer in existence
And fireworks became so much more
Than a visual experience.

Others may have touched my lips with theirs,
But not one has kissed them before.

- First Kiss

Love And Light

Heartbreak.
To experience death
Whilst breathing.

Joe Pound

If I could go back in time,
I would go back to when
The grooves of your clitorous
Were still embedded in my tongue.

- Come Home

Love And Light

It was in the darkness of her skin
Where I started
To see the light.

I am not a writer,

I am simply a transcriber.

Translating your existence into words.

Love And Light

I've always wondered why people who call someone
Who desires love.
Intimacy.
And
Affection.
A 'hopeless' romantic.

If anything,
Those people are hopeful romantics.
The people who have loved.
Lost.
And
Loved again.
Those who refuse to be scarred by their past.

How on earth can that be hopeless?

- Hopeful Romantic

Joe Pound

Love is why I write,
Love is why I live.

Love is why I take,
Love is why I give.

Through thick and thin.

Through stormy seas or sunny beaches.

Through depression or elation.

Through success or failure.

Through love or pain.

I'll be there.

- A Letter To Self

The.

Wealth.

Of.

Gold.

Will.

Never.

Equate.

To.

The.

Wealth.

Of.

Love.

- Consume Love, Not Products

Love And Light

There will always be someone better looking than you.
Stronger than you.
Faster than you.
More intelligent.

But there will never be anyone who can own the spot
Where you're standing,
Breathe the air your breathing
Or live in your skin,
Other than you.

You are you.
What a blessing.

Joe Pound

A B C D E F G H I J K L M N _ P Q R S T _ V W X _ Z

YOU.

All I need.

Love And Light

I need you like I need water;
Not out of thirst,
But because
You are a
Key component
Of
Keeping.
Me.
Alive.

Joe Pound

You struggled yesterday.

You may struggle today.

But by no means will you struggle tomorrow.

Don't allow pain to shadow your greatness.

Love And Light

Having you,
Having everything.

Don't let someone into your life

That's eager to hear your rhyme

Without having understood your first line.

- Patience

Love And Light

When you're feeling weak,
Breathe deep,
Repeat.

I am strong.
I am courageous.
I am love.

Joe Pound

I'm full without eating,
Having dreams without sleeping.

- Thank You

Love And Light

All I ever wanted to be was water,
All she ever wanted to be was fire.

I doused her flame,
Whilst she evaporated me.

We were everything,
Reduced to nothing.

Single we are droplets.
Together we are oceans.

- Unity

Love And Light

I was hungry,

So I put her in her place.

Where she belongs.

My face.

Joe Pound

Too many take

Love for granted

After their wish

For love has been granted.

- Inhale, Digest, Nurture

Love And Light

Even during a storm
I am able
To feel
The sun.

- Acceptance

The Kings crown
Can never compare to
The Queens throne.

- Royalty

Wealth.

Does.

Not.

Come.

In.

A.

Pay check.

Know when to be patient.
Know when you're wasting your time.

- Thin Line

Love And Light

You.
Will.
Never.
Live.
A.
Rich.
Life.
If.
Money.
Is.
Your.
Core.
Focus.

Joe Pound

It is always easier to criticise

Those who have burnt their fingers

When you are at a safe distance

From the flames.

Love And Light

My pen is my tongue
And I can't wait
To write poetry
Through your moans.

Joe Pound

Some are trapped by their minds,
Others are trapped by life's design.

Some are trapped by neither,
Yet still choose to live life blind.

Love And Light

I would call you beautiful,
But it wouldn't begin to describe
A fraction of the
Heavenly sent perfection
That you are.

Joe Pound

There was a melody in her lips,
A sweet samba in her kiss.

It was then that I realised
That even though I didn't move a single step,
Her lips had me dancing.

Love And Light

I told her that she was
The most beautiful creation
To ever grace this planet…

…She knew I wanted that ass.

Joe Pound

Love.
The be all.

War.
The end all.

Love And Light

Pens will always have a bigger impact than guns.

Where a gun's impact may leave you dead,
A pen's impact will leave you feeling alive.

Joe Pound

Family:
Related by blood,
But more so,
Related by love.

You were nothing but my girl.
I was everything but your man.

- Sorry

Joe Pound

The problem is,

People are too afraid to die

And not courageous enough to live.

- Do It

Love And Light

I have no recollection of sleeping
And I know not if I'm awake.

My dreams have become reality
And reality has become my dreams.

- Dazed And In Love

Joe Pound

Infatuation may move people
And faith may move mountains,
But our love
Can move worlds.

People are calling me *lucky*
Because I have found my 'one in a million'.

However,
I cannot agree that I am either lucky or that I've found
My 'one in a million'
Because I am *blessed*
To have found my 'one in seven billion'.

Joe Pound

If you know who you are
And you are who you want to be,
You may have experienced the most
Liberating discovery of your life.

Love And Light

I don't think you ever truly understood how
Much you meant to me.

Come to think of it,
I don't think I ever took the time
To let you know.

- Too Late

Joe Pound

You may be someone who I used to know,
But I am someone who you have never known.
You had no desire to learn who *I* was.

- Listen And Learn Me

Love And Light

We all have struggles in life,
So why not make our struggles worthwhile?

Struggle for your passions and desires.
Cry.
Fight.
Strive.
And
Bleed for them.

Give your struggles meaning,
You owe it to yourself.

Propel yourself into a journey
Where each new step
Will give you a better understanding
Of your own reality.

- Consciousness

Love And Light

There will never be enough
Time,
Words,
Or
Places
For
You
And
I.

- Eternal Day Dream

Joe Pound

I'd rather ride 1,000 storms with you
Than feel the sunshine with someone else.

Love And Light

I kissed you before I knew you,
I touched you before I grew with you.
I
  Lost
    You
      Before
        I
          Had
            You.

- Slope

Joe Pound

WAKE UP!
Because Ironically,
Dreams don't manifest
In feathered pillows.

Love And Light

A touch from the wrong person
Will solely be physical.
With the right person,
Physicality resembles the smallest
Aspect of a touch.

Joe Pound

You may not realise,

But you may only be one chapter away

From finishing your book.

You are too close to quit.

Don't.

Give.

Up.

Love And Light

Your lipstick may have washed from my lips,
But I can still taste your tarnish
From last nights memory.

- Flavour Of Sin

Joe Pound

How could I ever be sad when I'm not with you?

I have you in the morning sun,

The ocean waves

And the birds song.

- A Constant Presence

Love And Light

She was always a hidden sidewalk
Where no one dared to venture.

But one day she shall realise that
The road less travelled
Will always contain the greatest treasure.

- K.C.I.

You have allowed no space for my lips
And for that reason
I have to go.
I can sense that you're still full
From another's kisses.

- Lips For Rent

Love And Light

One small fire burning
Is of greater worth than a large pile
Of stacked wood.

Don't simply plan your journey,
Be on your journey.

- Ignite Your Flame

Perhaps I don't belong to the inner circles of love.
I will always be a great supporter.
An advocate.

But when my number is called
And I stand inside the arena
With the one I admire,
I buckle under pressure.

I love love.
Adore love.
Breathe love.

But not the responsibility that comes
With an intimate relationship.

- Honesty

In certain deaths
We are born.

- New Beginnings

Silence is precious.

The most valuable way to talk to someone is

Always through silence.

Speak to others through grace.

Humility.

Understanding.

Love.

And

Kindness.

Through your silence,

They will certainly hear you.

Love And Light

Love.
Over said,
Under practiced.

Joe Pound

The echo of your words within the stillness of the night

Is of a magical combination.

But just like a magician,

Your secrets may remain hidden.

I will pick and present all the stars for you

If that's what it will take

For you to reveal your

Mysteries to me.

- Krystal

Love And Light

We all belong in love.
Make no mistake about that.

If you're not in love.
Surrounded by love.
Or
Breathing love.
Hold tight.

Love is always around the corner.

Joe Pound

Don't be so shallow that people can easily paddle in you.
Be of depth,
So you will know
The select few that
Possess the strength
To explore your oceans.

Love And Light

And that's when I experienced the sweetest kiss.

When the ink from my pen
Met the paper of my notebook.

Little did I know that it would be the beginning
Of an ever-lasting relationship.

Joe Pound

Suddenly the strength of the wind was unbearable.
My heart was taken.
I was swept.

Love And Light

I love it when people love themselves.

Their crooked curves.

Uneven skin.

Rounded thighs.

Yes,

They see flaws,

But still come out smiling.

How disgustingly beautiful.

Joe Pound

I forgave you,
But in doing so,
I could never forgive myself.

- Self-harm

Fail.

Fail.

Fail.

Fail.

Fail.

Fail.

Fail.

Fail.

Fail.

Fail.

Fail.

Fail.

Fail.

Fail.

Fail.

Fail.

Succeed.

- Passion And Perseverance

Joe Pound

Made in the USA
Charleston, SC
30 November 2015